Aleida

a woman for the new millennium

Vladdo

Aleida
a woman for the new millennium

❊ PROLOGUE BY EDUARDO ARIAS ❊

❊ TRANSLATED BY PEDRO SHAIO ❊

Villegas
editores

©Vladimir Flórez —Vladdo
©Villegas Editores
Avenida 82 no. 11-50, interior 3
e-mail: villedi@cable.net.co
Telephone: (57-1) 616 1788. Fax (57-1) 616 0020
Bogotá, D.C., Colombia.

www.villegaseditores.com

Cover design and interior pages: Vladdo
Layout: Vladdo Danilo Black Asociados S.A.

Printing and binding in Colombia by Quebecor Impreandes

ISBN: 958-9393-94-2

First edition: October 2000

For Sofia, my daughter, who has taught me a new way of going bonkers over women.

A pebble in a man's shoe

Eduardo Arias

T o fall in love with her, seeing her just once is enough. Reclining, dressed, full-length, with a glass in her hand, her arms around a great cushion... little does it matter. But sure, men are such cowards, that when we feel the sharp edge of her implacable line, the impulse is to flee.

For we men can't stand being told truths, much less so if they are dolled up as aphorisms, graffitti or plays on words–all of which show us up. And even less so, if they emerge from a mouthless face that has no need to speak up, since these recurrent proofs of the stupidity of the masculine gender, even when whispered and barely perceptible, racket about forever in our minds.

Since she has no mouth, we will never know if she means what she says or is musing out loud, if she is serious, joking or just getting her rocks off pure and simple. This hermetic quality lapses only on the rare occasions when she lets slip a tear. Otherwise, she seems as changeless as the Sphinx.

She has the gift of being everywhere. One day she appears as a skeptical old maid, the next she is the disappointed bride, then the wife, resigned to the conjugal desert, and on the following day she poses as the dark side of a love triangle.

In any case, week after week we come back to her and try to understand what the devil she is hiding behind that enigmatic, implacable face—this two-dimensional being who is the product of the very few but precise lines of one of the great Colombian caricaturists of all times.

Vladdo, who made the big league with his magisterial saga of portraits of former president Virgilio Barco's government, and who has found, in the image of Andres Pastrana peeping out of a huge suit, a telling metaphor for the present administration's lack of leadership, has managed something quite difficult, for a man born and bred in a *machista* society like ours: to reflect the feminine spirit, which in Colombia we have nearly always put on the back burner and belittled.

Aleida, like a certain women one sees around, does not speak: she adjudicates. Now and again she comes out with some trite statement redolent of cant ("To say that guys are like dogs is to insult dogs.") which is sometimes all right. At other times she helplessly draws a sigh of longing for the loved one, and we think that now for sure we can dominate her, put her under our heel, keep her next to us to please us for the rest of our days. But it is merely a mirage, a trap she has set us, to have us believe that she is no longer capable of knocking us out. How naïve of us. The next broadside is lethal. A coldly considered change of punches that has us on the ropes yet again.

Possibly, for the *machistas* this country and the world are rife with, Aleida is a pebble in our shoe. Let's hope that this pebble is enough of a bother to make us stop and, once and for always, pay more attention to the female point of view, to that intuition that humankind needs so badly now, as it rushes toward the abyss under the stupid pretension of self-sufficiency of those who are strong, and rational—the *machos*.

Who is Aleida?

Vladdo

B iting, ardent, demure, naughty, disdainful passionate, critical, stylized...

Thus have people tried to define Aleida; but, while she has something of each of these qualities, none manages to capture her personality. She is unpredictable—being a woman—and therein lies her charm. When you expect gaiety, she's depressed; when you think she's going to be weak, she rises invincible; when you think her chaste, she's horny. She's that unusual...

There has also been more than one attempt to discover where her wit comes from and the origin of her ideas and the things she says. Because it's her, this is another thing that is hard to pin down. Her ideas might be the fruit of the love she has felt, the passions she has experienced, the disappointments she has endured, the drinks she has thrown back, the infidelities she has withstood, things she has read, guys she has suffered, songs she has heard or confidences made to her.

Another mystery lies in her physical appearance. Who is the source of inspiration for her, where do her clothes come from, why are her eyes that color, etc.? People ask if she is based on a real woman. A friend of Vladdo's perhaps? Or his wife? Or some famous person he knows?... All I can say is that she does indeed resemble some of the women I have known—both in her looks and the things she says—but, in fact, she is her own inspiration, lives in her own world and has her own way of thinking. Hers is a very special personality.

I n the end, what really matters is not whether she has got a line here or a kink there but that Aleida is the subjective and arbitrary opinion of a man who enjoys and suffers from women.

IT SEEMS
EASIER TO FIND
A CURE FOR AIDS
THAN ONE
FOR VIOLENCE

Vladdo

BEFORE, I'D GET JEALOUS
NOW I HAVE
A LOVER

Vladdo

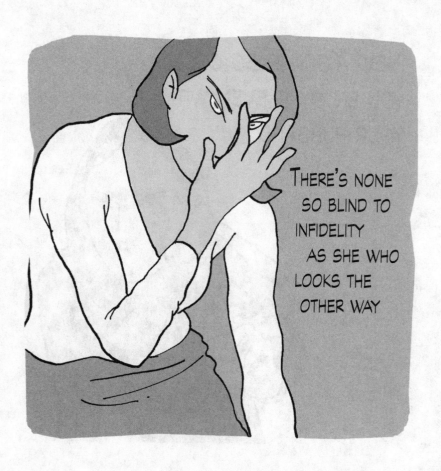

New York is so cool, you enjoy it even with your husband

A FAITHFUL GUY = A WOMAN
WHO KEEPS HER EYES OPEN

HOTLINES
BRING IT ALL DOWN TO
ORAL SEX

Vladdo

WHAT'S 'BAD'
ABOUT SEX IS
JUST WHAT'S
SO GOOD
ABOUT IT

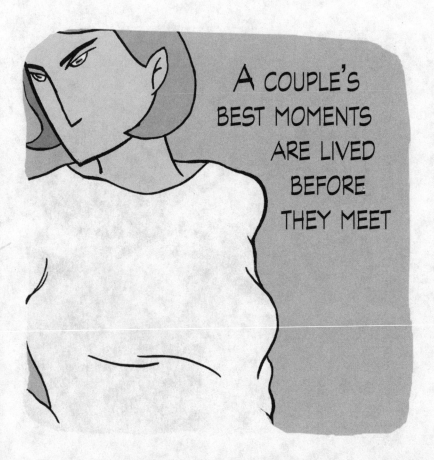

A COUPLE'S BEST MOMENTS ARE LIVED BEFORE THEY MEET

I SHOULD HAVE KNOWN THIS
LOVE TRIANGLE WOULD TURN OUT
WRONG...

BUT THEN
I ALWAYS **WAS**
BAD AT
GEOMETRY

Vladdo

EXPECTING THE LEAST
FROM A MAN
IS ALREADY
TO EXPECT TOO MUCH

WHOEVER SAID
IT WAS BETTER
TO BE ALONE
THAN IN BAD COMPANY
WAS A JERK

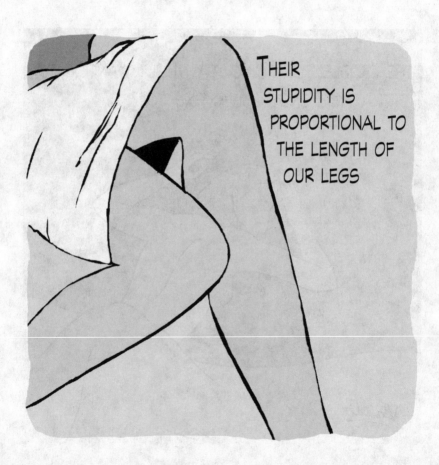

COMPARED TO A MAN, THE ADVANTAGE OF THE INTERNET IS THAT I ONLY HOOK UP WHEN I FEEL LIKE IT

THE WORST SIDE EFFECT OF AIDS IS DISCRIMINATION